ISO 9001: 2015

A Pocket Guide

ISO 9001: 2015

A Pocket Guide

Steve Watkins and Nick Orchiston

IT Governance Publishing

IT Governance Publishing
IT Governance Limited
Unit 3, Clive Court
Bartholomew's Walk
Cambridgeshire Business Park
Ely, Cambridgeshire
CB7 4EA
United Kingdom

www.itgovernance.co.uk

First published in the United Kingdom in 2016
by IT Governance Publishing.

ISBN 978-1-84928-811-8

ABOUT THE AUTHORS

Steve G Watkins has been working with quality management standards since the days of BS 5750, first applying it in a leisure centre and then other service sector environments. In addition to quality, his experience includes environment, health and safety, information security, business continuity, and IT service management systems, working with the relevant British and international standards. Steve sits on a number of UK technical committees that contribute to ISO's work developing and revising standards in the areas of risk, information security and service management. He also contracts to UKAS as a technical assessor, giving him a strong understanding of accredited certification.

Nick Orchiston is a management systems consultant with more than 20 years' experience encompassing quality (ISO 9001), health & safety (OHSAS 18001), environmental (ISO 14001), IT service management (ITIL/ISO 20000) and information security (ISO 27001) management systems. He has successfully supported a wide variety of organisations, from SMEs to global corporations, through to accredited certification to all of these standards. Nick also created the IT Governance Toolkits for ISO 9001, ISO 14001, ISO 16001, ISO 50001, and OHSAS 18001 standards, used across the globe by project implementers.

CONTENTS

Contents

INTRODUCTION

All organisations supply goods or provide services – it is simply the nature of the world; an elegant demonstration of quid pro quo, as it were. Of course, many go about their business assuming that as long as they continue to be able to do so, they will continue to do business.

This model relies on the organisation always being able to provide goods and services to at least the minimum standard that the market is willing to accept. For some industries, this minimum standard is extremely high – luxury goods, for instance, or industries in which high standards are essential, such as precision instruments. Even for organisations operating in markets with very low minimum standards, it's obvious that there's a point below which the market will no longer support the business.

Every organisation should know what their minimum standard that supports continuance is, and they must be able to provide it. For some organisations, this means setting their minimum standard well above the minimum that their market will tolerate, thereby allowing a margin of error. If you cannot consistently deliver products and services that meet your customers' expectations, you'll soon find yourself not doing business with anyone.

Equally, there is a maximum standard, beyond which the organisation doesn't want to improve the product or service. This is the level at which the investment in achieving that standard no longer delivers a satisfactory return, either because the market doesn't want to pay more, or because the organisation cannot afford the additional investment. However, the desire to find a more effective, efficient and ultimately economical manner of achieving this level or standard of product or service remains.

Understanding this dynamic is the foundation of quality management.

Management systems

ISO 9001:2015 is the internationally recognised standard for quality management systems. A quality management system (QMS) is a framework organisations use to ensure consistent results when designing, developing and delivering products and services.

Management systems have been developed to manage a range of different business disciplines, and each comes with its own specific benefits. Following a management system standard, such as those produced by the International Organization for Standardization (ISO), has the additional benefit that its uptake means that it's more likely to be recognised and understood by clients, partners and suppliers.

Critically, management system standards are general: they can be applied to any organisation, in any industry, anywhere in the world. Rather than dictating specific tools, they describe processes and functions that any organisation can follow to improve the given management discipline. For organisations that might have been operating for some time, this can be comforting – the longer a business runs, the more likely it is to have established its own form of management system, and to have encountered and implemented good practice. For these businesses, moving from a sort of organic, ad hoc management system to one that is holistic, consistent and formalised, the process could be described as cathartic.

Therefore, a management system based on an ISO standard provides two immediate benefits: the ability to implement a system based on accepted good practice, and, through the associated accredited certification scheme, a means of recognising conformity with that good practice.

CHAPTER 1: WHAT IS A QUALITY MANAGEMENT SYSTEM?

Although it would be simple to describe a quality management system (QMS) as a system for managing quality, that's not a useful definition (and would be justly rejected by any dictionary). More usefully, a QMS is a set of interacting policies, objectives and processes designed to make sure that quality requirements for products and services are met.[1] These requirements can be set either internally (the organisation's criteria) or externally (customers', and others', requirements). Crucially, it should be seen as including an organisational structure – including appropriate authorities, responsibilities and accountabilities, along with the required competences for each – rather than a set of simple processes and requirements.

It is also important to remember that a QMS can be applied to both products *and* services. For businesses that focus on only products or services, this may appear to be a redundant point, but it's important to recall that many businesses provide both, even if they don't realise it. A company that sells products online, for instance, is implicitly offering their webshop as a service. The customer isn't buying the webshop, but it has an inherent value reflected in repeat customers, multiple purchases and so on.

Quality management should be a primary focus for any organisation. Regardless of the level of investment actually put into the product or service, ensuring a minimum 'rejection' level is simply good business. Although almost every organisation recognises this, approaches to quality management can be incredibly varied. In its simplest form, the product or service is subject to quality control – someone looks at the product or service and assesses whether it meets the organisation's

---

[1] See ISO 9000:2015, 3.5.3 and 3.5.4 for the formal ISO definitions.

established criteria. For some products, there may not even be established quality criteria beyond 'it does not break'. An equivalent criterion for services might be 'it isn't awful to work with'.

This is reactive quality management (also called quality control): the product or service has already been produced before it is checked for conformance. The problem with reactive quality management is that you might produce thousands of widgets before passing a sample to quality control, only to discover that a significant proportion aren't up to scratch and hundreds of widgets require rework – or worse – disposal. It's better than no quality management at all, but it doesn't give the organisation significant benefits.

Proactive quality management, on the other hand, establishes methods of designing, producing and delivering products and services so that results are consistent. Assuming your processes are effective, your products and services will meet the expected standards. This is much like a machine in a factory being set to achieve the required output from the outset: the machine performs a series of actions that result in converting one object into another object, repeatedly and consistently to meet requirements.

Obviously, some part of quality management must be reactive – it would be foolish to rely on proactive measures to get everything right and simply send out your widgets without checking that the processes worked as intended, no matter how confident you are in your quality assurance arrangements. Equally, following the factory machine analogy, some maintenance is required: the machine must be cleaned, blades sharpened, parts replaced and so on, and the processes must also be re-examined, tidied and improved.

And, of course, all of this relies on *people following the defined processes*. The path of least resistance is always the most appealing, and this often means cutting corners, fudging complexities and generally finding easier ways to do things. Although it would be nice if we could come up with processes that are immune to this (although assembly line methodologies are intended to be), in many cases this will not be possible because of the demands of the product or service.

So, an effective QMS uses proactive processes to determine how each stage of a product or service's production cycle is performed, and reactive processes to check that this was done correctly. The two approaches complement each other to improve efficiency and quality.

Aside from ensuring that investments make it through to delivery, quality correlates with customer satisfaction. The importance of customer satisfaction cannot be understated, especially regarding the QMS.

Satisfaction is based on the product or service meeting the customer's needs, not necessarily the simple fact that it does what you design it to do – it's even possible that the product or service meets a need that it wasn't intended for. Because quality and satisfaction are so closely related, satisfaction essentially becomes an important metric of quality.

This relationship can operate as a feedback loop: rather than designing the product or service to meet arbitrary quality objectives, it can be designed to meet customers' needs. This may seem obvious – after all, who doesn't design their products and services to meet their customers' requirements? Despite this apparent truism, it's important to keep in mind, as that objective can be lost when you're too familiar with your products and services. Just as we're all aware that products and services should meet customers' needs, we've all also heard internal complaints that customers "don't know what they want" and that "they're using [the product or service] wrong!"

Applying a standard

Although most organisations will have their own processes for ensuring the quality of their products and services, it can be useful to look for external guidance to make sure that your

QMS is the best it can be. As mentioned earlier, this is true of many business disciplines.

ISO standards provide a set of generic requirements for the organisation, which allows you to get all the key processes in place, as well as defining their relationships. This makes sure the organisation as a whole is on board and understands the management system's importance, and can be independently verified to assure partners, suppliers and customers of your organisation's credentials.

Furthermore, because ISO standards are based on tried and tested good practice, they essentially provide the collected wisdom of thousands of practitioners garnered over decades of experience. This is distilled into a few pages and sold for a relative pittance.

ISO 9001, like other ISO management system standards, specifies a management system that incorporates continual improvement, which ensures its ongoing value for the organisation. This way, even if the Standard isn't updated for several years – and it is unlikely to be – the organisation is in a position to adapt to changes such as manufacturing improvements, technologies and so on.

This is an important feature of the Standard, as it makes sure the QMS is flexible and adaptable, rather than imposing a rigid structure that might have been ideal for the organisation at a single moment in time. Establishing the QMS so that it can change with the nature of the business environment is essential.

CHAPTER 2: A BRIEF HISTORY OF QUALITY MANAGEMENT AND ISO 9001

The pursuit of quality and consistency goes back a long time – probably as long as trade has existed. A craftsman or merchant in the traditional mould wants their product to be the best fit to requirements that it can be so they can minimise costly reworking and ensure ongoing demand/funding. In pre-industrial societies, production was typically conducted by an individual responsible for all parts of the final product or service, so training and practising was by far the most common way to ensure quality.

When industrialisation arrived in the eighteenth century, the distribution of labour between both people and machines meant that traditional quality practices were no longer really effective or necessary. An employer didn't want to have to train someone to be good at their job when it was more useful to have them replaceable; rather, jobs were typically reduced to performing the smallest part of the whole, making the employee – like the machine – almost entirely replaceable.

In splitting labour up in this way, standardisation became an important aspect of manufacturing. At the turn of the nineteenth century, Eli Whitney popularised the use of interchangeable parts in muskets to reduce per-unit costs and increase the lifetime of the weapon (thereby also making notable contributions to cost accountancy).

Achieving true interchangeability naturally requires those parts to be standardised. To get this standardisation, you either need to have appropriately skilled workers, precision tools or easily replicated processes. Of the three options, the third is clearly the cheapest and simplest. Certainly, you can't guarantee exceptional quality with this method, but you can get consistent results and production can also be kept high without expensive equipment or highly trained employees.

This culminated in Henry Ford's improvement of the assembly line that reduced the worker's role almost to that of a cog in the machine, thereby reducing the time to build a car from 12 hours to merely 93 minutes. Goods could be produced quickly, efficiently, cheaply and – most importantly – to a consistent standard. Although Ford's innovations are generally seen as an advance in manufacturing technologies, the principles clearly fall within the realm of quality management.

Formalised quality management, however, is a relatively new phenomenon. It's older than many other business disciplines, but in the grander narrative of history it's positively youthful. The first formalised QMS was set out in MIL-Q-9858 in 1959, which was a description of quality programme requirements for military contractors in the US. Although it was updated several times, it was eventually replaced in 1996 in favour of supporting industry consensus standards rather than enforcing government directives.

This specification contained a great deal that is still relevant today: establishing workflows, controlling inputs and outputs, establishing quality objectives and so on. Rather than having been disproved or rendered redundant over the years, these fundamental points have evolved and been iterated upon.

While MIL-Q-9858 was in use, private industry had already begun developing codified processes for quality management. BS 5179 (released in 1974) was among the first, and is the clear predecessor to ISO 9001. Being developed as a national standard provided a great deal of attention and provided evidence and feedback, enabling the Standard to evolve further, into BS 5750 in 1979. Although BS 5179 had provided guidance on quality systems, it did not actually provide a specification for a QMS. This led many organisations to develop their own systems using the advice from BS 5179, but also led to difficulties in providing customers and business partners with appropriate assurance.

BS 5750 was the first standard to describe an actual QMS, which generated enough interest that ISO developed it as ISO 9001:1987. This has since been updated several times, in 1994, 2000, 2008 and 2015.

By 2000, there were 457,834 ISO 9001 certifications worldwide, which leapt to 1,118,510 by 2010. As of 2014, the growth had slowed, but it remains by far the most widely adopted ISO management system standard, with 1,138,155 certifications worldwide.[2] The Standard has traditionally been popular in Europe and Japan, but in recent years the BRIC nations have invested heavily in meeting the requirements of the specification, such that the Russian Federation, India and China now feature in the top ten (China, in fact, now accounts for about a quarter of all ISO 9001 certifications).

---

[2] All statistics from the ISO Survey, *www.iso.org/iso/home/standards/certification/iso-survey.htm*

CHAPTER 3: USEFUL DEFINITIONS

Although ISO standards aim for clear and concise language, some terms have specific definitions and ramifications for quality management. The Standard itself references ISO 9000:2015 for explanations of relevant terms and definitions, but some additional commentary is useful for clarity, especially if you are new to management systems in general.

Quality

As noted earlier, quality does not necessarily mean that a product or service is provided to the highest standard; rather, it means that it is provided to the standard that the organisation sees fit. As ISO 9000:2015 states, "The quality of an organization's products and services is determined by the ability to satisfy customers and the intended and unintended impact on relevant interested parties", which makes it a function of the organisation's ability to do business with its customers and other interested parties.

This naturally extends to the organisation's culture, since an organisation that does not value the quality of its products and services will be unlikely to maintain the processes necessary to achieve the purportedly desired levels of quality. As such, you should make sure that your organisation understands what quality means and how each person contributes to it.

Context of the organisation

Modern ISO management system standards require the organisation to take the 'context of the organisation' into account when implementing the management system. This is a broad idea, encompassing the organisation's business environment, industry, major partners and suppliers, legal requirements and so on. Essentially, the management system should not only fit the organisation itself but also be built with the broader environment in mind.

The idea of a business aligning its functions and processes with its objectives isn't new, so this should not be difficult to come to terms with. It is important to remember, however, that determining the context of the organisation doesn't necessarily need to be incredibly granular – a complete list of all interested parties isn't necessary, for instance, as that could be overwhelmingly vast for some organisations, and simply recording all of them would be a massive project in itself. Rather, the organisation should identify the most important factors to its context.

Furthermore, the context should consider what the organisation itself wants to achieve. It can be useful to think of this in idealised terms that the organisation itself uses, such as mission statements, vision, objectives and so on.

Documented information

Documented information is crucial to any management system, and comprises all forms of documentation: policies, procedures, work instructions, records and so on. It is important to remember that certification of the management system will rely on having both a structured management system and evidence that it is functioning. This evidence includes results of checks on the products and services, as well as the results of checks on the QMS itself.

In previous versions of the Standard, 'documents' and 'records' were treated separately. This is no longer the case, so all documented information is now bound by the same requirements.

Finally, it's very easy to forget that a management system is more than a set of documentation. Simply having all the required documents available isn't necessarily proof that your organisation has developed a management system. As ISO states: "It is stressed that ISO 9001 requires (and always *has* required) a

'Documented quality management system', and not a *'system of documents'*."[3]

As such, the documented information you choose to develop (or where your organisation's 'context' requires it) should be an accurate reflection of the actual quality processes you have in place. Developing this documentation should be collaborative, so that the actual process meets the requirements of the Standard, and that the documentation accurately describes the process in action, rather than the documentation describing something that meets the Standard but doesn't describe what actually happens.

Inputs and outputs

All business processes have inputs and outputs, so the terms should be or should soon become familiar to anyone looking to implement a formal management system. It's useful to remember, however, that inputs and outputs apply to all levels of the QMS – that is, the product or service has inputs and outputs, as do those processes that belong to the more abstract QMS.

Equally, inputs and outputs can take many forms. Understanding how to capture these so that they can be tracked and measured as necessary can present a logical puzzle. By staying aware of the importance of inputs and outputs when designing or formalising your QMS processes, it is much simpler to make sure that they are appropriately identified, measured and tracked.

Interested parties

Related to the earlier 'context of the organisation', interested parties are those people and organisations with some interest in

---

[3] Guidance on the requirements for Documented Information of ISO 9001:2015, www.iso.org/iso/ documented_information.pdf.

your organisation and its activities. By default, this will include customers and suppliers, regulatory bodies and so on.

In some instances, interested parties could go beyond what the organisation itself realises, with the definition in ISO 9000:2015 stating that it includes "person or organization that can affect, be affected by, or perceive itself to be affected by a decision or activity".[4] In the UK, for instance, the scale of the public sector is such that it would be almost negligent to assume that contracts with government bodies won't happen.[5] Because of this, additional considerations may be necessary relating to meeting quality standards specified by government departments that exceed legislated standards.

Products and services

In previous editions of the Standard, 'products' was specifically defined as including services. This is no longer the case, presumably in order to remind organisations that services should also be subject to quality management and to account for the fact that services now form a significant part of major economies.

Furthermore, services have some differences from products, notably in that the output is typically more difficult to measure before it reaches the customer. As such, organisations will need to make provisions to maximise quality in the design and development phases to make sure that services meet customer requirements.

---

[4] ISO 9000:2015, 3.2.3.
[5] Approximately 19% of the UK's workforce is employed in the public sector.

Risk-based thinking

This draws from experience of taking risk into account in other disciplines and is thoroughly described in the Standard's Annex A.4. It outlines the role that risk plays in making sure the organisation meets quality objectives, in particular in its role as preventive action; because the QMS itself is a preventive measure, risk must, therefore, play a central role.

'Risk' is the "effect of uncertainty" (sometimes described as the "effect of uncertainty on objectives"), which can be either positive or negative, although it is most frequently understood in negative terms. Risk represents potential events that have consequences for the organisation, which should either be planned for (to limit the effect and/or compensate when they occur) or prevented.

Annex A.4 makes it clear that the organisation is not compelled to implement a complete risk-assessment process for the QMS. Instead, the organisation should determine an appropriate level of risk awareness, whether that be through formal risk assessment, procedural consideration of risks or simply keeping risks in mind while implementing and managing the organisation's quality processes. The extent to which an organisation identifies risk awareness is required is likely to vary by the nature of the process(es) being considered.

CHAPTER 4: REQUIREMENTS OF
ISO 9001:2015

The Standard comprises ten clauses (eleven if you include the introduction – Clause 0), of which seven (Clauses 4–10) specify the requirements for a QMS. Clause 0 provides context for the Standard, including some guidance on how the PDCA cycle (Plan-Do-Check-Act) may be adopted and the principles of quality management. Clauses 1–3 describe the application of the Standard, the reference material that is essential in understanding and applying the standard, terms and definitions, and so on. The requirements are followed by a pair of annexes (A and B), which are informative (they provide additional information) rather than normative (indispensable for the application of the document, such as ISO 9000: effectively mandated reading!).

In many cases, the requirements of the Standard will already be met through existing processes. Checking and confirming which requirements are met can be a valuable process before beginning your implementation project, and can be achieved with a gap analysis.[6]

Although this book does not describe an implementation path or methodology, the commentary that follows will be useful for implementers to make sure that some of the finer details have been identified and met.

For organisations seeking assistance with their first ISO 9001 implementation, consultants can provide a range of services. Regardless of the level of service, the organisation can take

---

[6] A gap analysis checks the requirements against your current state. A gap analysis tool can be used to streamline this process by posing a set of questions that can be answered with a yes/no/qualified yes. These tools allow the organisation to quickly identify where work needs to be done.

advantage of a consultant's expertise to develop knowledge and skills relevant to the management system and thereby simplifying ongoing compliance.

Plan-Do-Check-Act

Subclause 0.3.2 describes the PDCA cycle, which is a recommended but not prescribed method of implementing, maintaining and continually improving an ISO 9001-compliant QMS.

Rather than just describing the methodology behind PDCA – which is widely understood – the Standard also provides a diagram to show how it works in relation to ISO 9001. This depicts the cycle as the operation of each of the clauses, with key inputs and outputs. It demonstrates that the cycle is not only applicable to the QMS, but also to product and service provision in general.

CHAPTER 5 – CONTEXT OF THE ORGANISATION

As described in the previous chapter, the context of the organisation is, broadly speaking, the environment in which the organisation does business, including the specific pressures affecting quality. The most tangible output of the Clause is the defined scope of the QMS. Although there is no requirement to progress through the clauses in order, this is clearly an important step early in the implementation of the QMS.

For an organisation to meet the requirements, it must be able to identify the key issues and stakeholders affecting quality. This can include the availability of resources, economic realities, customers and suppliers, legal and regulatory considerations, and so on. Although the organisation does not need to enumerate every single factor impacting quality, it does need to be able to identify its requirements for quality based on those pressures.

This clause takes an abstract perspective and includes the overarching requirement, at 4.4, to "establish, implement, maintain and continually improve a quality management system". This includes establishing the broad structure of the QMS and the interaction between its processes.

Finally, the QMS processes should be documented where there may be doubt that the process will consistently produce quality products and services. As such, the QMS is both a record of what the organisation claims to do and a record of what the organisation actually does. Any organisation implementing ISO 9001 should make sure that these align.

Clause 5 – Leadership

This clause is directed almost solely at "top management", which is the "person or group of people who directs and controls an organization at the highest level".[7] This focus makes sure that the QMS is led by individuals able to provide the resources and authority to establish, implement, maintain and improve the management system. Furthermore, because the QMS should integrate with the organisation's broader business objectives and strategic direction, top management involvement is essential.

It should be noted that the "highest level" may not actually be the leader of the organisation and their peers – a QMS that only covers a portion of the organisation, for instance, can be led by the highest authority for that part of the organisation, rather than defaulting to the Board of Directors or C-suite executives.

Customer focus is directly addressed within the Clause, which reflects the fact that quality is a function of the product or service's ability to meet customers' requirements. The fact that this is addressed through leadership implies that the organisation should take this seriously – one of the aims of an ISO 9001 conforming QMS is that it enables the organisation to consistently provide products and services that meet customer requirements.

Top management must also produce a quality policy, which declares the organisation's dedication to and perspective on quality. It also provides a framework for establishing the quality objectives that the QMS aims to fulfil. The policy doesn't need to be a lengthy document – the requirements for the policy are actually quite brief – but it does need to be communicated and available to "relevant interested parties, as appropriate".

Although the requirements dedicated to the quality policy are relatively brief, it's important to remember that the policy should provide a framework for setting quality objectives. These are not necessarily the objectives for the QMS, but are specific to a

---

[7] ISO 9000:2015, 3.1.1.

function, level or process within the organisation. For instance, quality objectives might be reducing the rejection rate at a certain stage in production, or increasing human productivity (as opposed to machine productivity); QMS objectives might be reducing the total rejection rate to a defined level, improving sales through greater customer satisfaction, or meeting a contractual obligation to achieve accredited certification to ISO 9001.

Finally, top management is required to assign appropriate roles, responsibilities and authorities relating to quality and the QMS. As is repeatedly asserted, this includes responsibilities and authorities for making sure the QMS operates as intended and conforms to the requirements of ISO 9001, as well as the more obvious responsibilities and authorities for performing quality processes.

Clause 6 – Planning

This clause is focused on risk, quality objectives and change, which are interrelated functions within the QMS. In other words, risks can influence quality objectives – either through threatening them or becoming the topic of a quality objective – and change management makes sure that the organisation can adapt to the needs of the risks and the quality objectives.

Addressing risks and opportunities, as described in the previous chapter, does not necessarily take the form of a risk assessment. Whatever process the organisation adopts, it should be prepared to demonstrate how risk-based thinking is integrated into its processes, whether that be through the auditor interviewing personnel, reviewing notes of risk-related discussions at meetings or any other means.

Subclause 6.1 recalls the role that internal and external issues (as discussed in Clause 4) play in determining how quality is managed, as well as the requirements of interested parties. It is possible that these issues and requirements place stresses on the organisation that present risks to quality – or present opportunities. The possibility that opportunities arise is often overshadowed by the fear of the negative risks, so establishing a path for the recognition of opportunities can be a valuable investment.

It may be useful to think of this process in terms of making sure that it meets its quality objectives (by addressing risks) and can achieve continual improvement (by recognising and acting on opportunities). Thinking of it in this way aligns the clause with the broader goals of the QMS, rather than being seen as a requirement that adds burden without benefit.

Subclause 6.2 establishes the requirements for quality objectives and for plans to achieve them.

One of the more critical points is making sure that the objectives are measurable. This allows the organisation to inform the focus of future resources most appropriately, prove that they are meeting the requirements of ISO 9001 and also to prove that their actions are having the desired effects on quality.

While Clause 6.3 could be considered part of continual improvement – and in many ways it is – it can also be applied to make changes when no improvement is explicitly occurring. That is, some changes may be necessary without being designed specifically to deliver improvement of (or weakening, ideally) the QMS. Such changes might include adjusting the scope of the management system, accounting for changes in the business' structure and so on.

Clause 7 – Support

Supporting the QMS by providing the necessary resources and organisational structures is critical to the success of any management system. The Standard broadly divides support into resources, competence, awareness, communication and documented information. Resources and competence are closely related, as are awareness and communication, and documented information should encompass nearly every facet of the management system.

It is important to note that all forms of support should be available and relevant to all stages of the QMS: establishment, implementation, maintenance and continual improvement. It can be easy to forget this and fail to allocate suitable resources beyond the initial implementation – if you are adopting the PDCA cycle, it is relevant well beyond the planning stage.

The requirements around resource in the Standard are particularly thorough, covering people, infrastructure, environment in which the processes are operated, measuring and organisational knowledge. For most organisations, this is simply part of everyday business – making sure resources are available for business processes shouldn't be a surprise – but it's useful to have a codified set of requirements for quality processes in particular, not least because the Standard may highlight important features that are not reflected in your current processes.

The aspect relating to monitoring and measuring is particularly noteworthy – the management information this generates helps focus future effort more appropriately.

Following resources, the Standard lays out the requirements for competence. The organisation should establish methods of identifying the actual requirements, assessing whether the appropriate individuals meet those requirements, and how to develop the necessary competence if it is not currently available. Once a competence is identified as required, it should be taken into account when hiring or assessing existing staff, and making it part of the business as a whole.

Competence is assessed on the basis of education, training or experience, ensuring those involved have the "ability to apply knowledge and skills to achieve intended results".[8] It is

---

[8] ISO 9000:2015, 3.10.4

dangerous to rely on a single individual having the competence to do certain work if finding a replacement is going to be near impossible because of that individual's curious combination of three degrees, 17 years' experience in a niche field and a host of certifications from programmes that no longer exist. Even in less absurd situations, it's more than useful to be able to train staff or hire contractors for busy periods, absence and the like.

Requirements for awareness apply to all "persons doing work under the organization's control", which can include people who are not ordinary employees of the organisation, such as contractors, suppliers' employees and so on. The organisation must make sure that all such people are aware of key information regarding the aspects of the QMS they are required to adhere to, which serves to inform everyone of the importance of quality management and to make it part of everyday business.

Communication requirements in Subclause 7.4 cover both internal and external communications, although additional requirements for internal communication are also present elsewhere in the Standard (such as the requirements for communicating the quality policy, in Subclause 5.2.2). Defining communication procedures should not be difficult, and simply formalises what most organisations already do.

Subclause 7.5 describes the requirements for documented information. This is one of the more demanding parts of the Standard because many organisations don't document their processes or take the time to properly manage what documentation they do keep. Furthermore, because a QMS can be a very large project, this can also mean creating and updating a great deal of documentation. It is also important to remember that the organisation needs to keep the documentation required by the Standard as well as the evidence it needs to be sure that the QMS is effective.

Many of the documentation requirements are common to all ISO management system standards, so it's valuable to implement these requirements as broadly as you can, even beyond the scope of the

QMS. This will make sure that all documentation is handled consistently and following good practice requirements.

There are no requirements for the format or medium of your organisation's documentation – a set of diagrams printed on paper and kept in a folder is just as valid as electronic files stored on a company intranet, as long as the documents meet the requirements of ISO 9001 and the organisation's needs.

If you're daunted by the scale of documentation necessary, it may be useful to seek out a documentation toolkit containing templates of all the necessary documents.[9] The key to getting the most from any documentation toolkit is to bespoke the templates as much as necessary to make them fit your organisation's context, objectives and business.

Another key requirement for documentation is that it is appropriately identified, reviewed, approved and controlled. Establishing processes to manage this makes sure that the organisation's documentation is readily located, accurate and – crucially – known to be accurate.

The organisation must also determine how that documentation is accessed and handled. Not all documentation needs to be available to all staff, whereas other documents (such as the quality policy) will need to be broadly accessible. This includes determining how the documentation is stored, preserved and disposed of: does your documentation need to be destroyed or archived? Are there legal considerations or a need to protect the information from prying eyes?

---

[9] Documentation toolkits typically provide all the mandatory documents for a given management system, as well as a set of raw templates for generic documentation (such as work instructions, records and so on). Better documentation toolkits will also come with a set of ancillary tools to help you verify whether you have met the requirements, as well as guidance documentation to help you understand specific elements of the implementation and the standard.

It is useful to reiterate here that a QMS should be a functioning, appropriately documented management system, not a system of documents. Simply having documents describing what you should be doing is not enough in itself to bring the benefits of a QMS; the organisation needs to make sure that any QMS documents describe what you actually do, and that what you are actually doing is sufficient to meet your quality objectives.

Clause 8 – Operation

Clause 8 contains by far the most requirements in the Standard, which is to be expected: responsibility for quality largely resides in the organisation's day-to-day operations. The requirements cover the whole lifecycle of products and services, so each step has processes in place to meet quality requirements.

These processes will generally be generic so that they can be applied to any product or service that the organisation provides, whereas the work instructions, if deemed necessary, for actually producing the product/service will necessarily be more precise and specific.

Operational planning and control is outlined in Subclause 8.1, and essentially provides the minimum requirements for all processes and actions that are part of day-to-day operations of the organisation. Notably, these requirements also apply to the implementation of actions determined in Clause 6 (actions to address risks and opportunities). It also involves controlling processes to make sure they meet criteria established for those processes – and that this occurs for outsourced processes, too.

The subclauses that follow this broadly track the progression of a product or service from its initial conception through to post-delivery activities.

Subclause 8.2 outlines how the organisation determines the requirements for products and services. This includes communicating with customers on a number of topics, including information about products and services, obtaining feedback and complaints, and so on.

The organisation needs to identify the requirements for products and services according to a number of specific pressures, including customers' requirements. These pressures also include statutory and regulatory requirements, requirements deemed necessary by the organisation, and making sure that the organisation can actually deliver the product or service as described.

The latter half of this subclause makes sure that the requirements for products and services have been accurately identified. This is handled in two separate processes: the first is for the review and confirmation of the product/service requirements, and the second accounts for changes to those requirements. Obviously, it is best if the review is thorough enough so that later changes are not necessary, but this may not always be possible. As such, having a backup process in place to allow changes to be made retroactively is both sensible and useful.

With the requirements for products and services set in place, Subclause 8.3 describes the requirements for processes involved in the design and development of products and services to meet those requirements. Different products and services will have different needs for design and development, however, so the Standard leaves the general structure of this process open to the organisation, instead making sure that the process is appropriately planned, that controls are in place, and that inputs and outputs are identified for each stage.

Planning of design and development processes (Subclause 8.3.2) defines the requirements for preparing ahead of the development work. This could be standardised across all the organisation's products and services, but it is more sensible to create a process that determines the appropriate phases according to the needs of the product or service.

The subsequent phases for design and development relate to the inputs, controls, outputs and changes. Inputs are the information, content, resources and so on that the organisation enters into the design and development process, and outputs are the expected results. This also needs to include appropriate outputs for confirming that quality requirements are being met, such as metrics that can be fed to the monitoring and measurement processes (which will be discussed in Clause 9).

To make sure that the design and development process works as intended, the organisation needs to apply appropriate controls. Some such controls can be seen as preliminary monitoring and measurement activities, and others are proactive measures to prevent errors from occurring, validating that the emerging blueprints are aligning with the identified, and potentially changing, requirements.

Although changes to design and development are common – as anyone involved in the process can attest – the organisation needs to correctly manage these changes to ensure that the requirements will still be met. Subclause 8.3.6 also makes it clear that the process should ensure there is no adverse impact versus the requirements and sets specific requirements for documented information relating to changes.

Subclause 8.4 relates to externally provided processes, products and services.

Most organisations will already have processes in place to manage quality from external suppliers, although it's likely that the processes are inconsistently applied, informal and undocumented. A sense of the requirements in this section of ISO 9001 can be conveyed by asking a few questions:

• Do the processes/products/services meet our requirements? Can we make sure they do so consistently?

Subclause 8.4.1 requires the organisation to identify how the organisation checks whether each supplier's goods and services are appropriate for its needs. As such, the organisation needs to make sure that its requirements are clear (8.4.3) and comprehensible so that suppliers cannot be under any illusions as to what the organisation wants.

This subclause also requires the organisation to have an established set of criteria for selecting and managing suppliers.

Subclause 8.4.2 is subtly different from 8.4.1 in that it establishes controls to make sure that supplied processes, products and services align with its quality requirements. This is an extension of the previous subclause, in the sense that supplier-provided processes, products and services can have an impact on the organisation's ability to deliver. Such concerns might include making sure suppliers can reliably deliver on time, that software will not introduce unexpected consequences, that a particular product is provided within a specific narrow tolerance, and so on.

Subclause 8.4.3 is a set of requirements for a practice that almost every organisation will already have in place. The subclause requires the organisation to communicate with its suppliers regarding requirements for quality verification/validation.

Subclause 8.5 outlines the controls that organisations should put in place for product and service realisation. The first subclause within this – Control of production and service provision – appears to include a delivery function (service provision). Although you might expect to see this as part of Subclause 8.6 (Release of products and services), it is properly placed here as service provision is directly analogous to production. Furthermore, the controls described relate more to the functionalities involved in providing a service (infrastructure and so on) than the release of that service. The release of products and services at 8.6 is more akin to the sign-off of the product/service before release/launch.

Because production and service provision can be a lengthy phase in the broader process, Subclause 8.5.2 requires the organisation to identify and trace appropriate outputs. Some such outputs will be relevant for monitoring and measurement purposes, and others will be various stages of the product or service that can be tested for conformity to requirements.

Subclause 8.5.3 is a slightly expanded version of 2008's Subclause 7.5.4 – Customer property. 2015's standard now recognises that organisations may equally need to establish rules and controls to account for providers' property as well as customers'. In other regards, this requirement should mesh with most organisations' ordinary procedures for handling external parties' property.

Although it may appear little more than a sort of reminder, Subclause 8.5.4 is an important requirement in the Standard. The subclause requires the organisation to preserve outputs during production and service provision, which makes sure that there is an auditable trail following the product/service through its production lifecycle. Trails like this make sure that the organisation can pinpoint the stage at which nonconformities occur.

The post-delivery activities described in Subclause 8.5.5 should be developed before the product or service has actually been released. In some cases, this may be because of safety concerns – such as making sure that a product is accompanied by training – or other legally mandated requirements, whereas in other instances it is simply to make sure that your organisation gathers feedback on the quality of the product/service from the most relevant source: the customer.

When releasing products and services, Subclause 8.6 requires the organisation to have arrangements in place to check (and recheck) that the product/service meets quality requirements. As this is traditionally the last chance you have to make sure your customer receives the quality they expect, this is an important – if unsurprising – requirement. Of note, the organisation is required to establish accountability for the release by making sure that the person(s) who authorised it can be traced.

The final subclause in Clause 8 lays out the requirements for controlling outputs that do not meet requirements.

Clause 9 – Performance evaluation

There are three core practices involved in performance evaluation: monitoring, measurement, analysis and evaluation; internal audit; and management review. The first two determine how well the organisation's QMS is operating and where nonconformities are occurring, and the management review assesses all of this information to drive corrective actions and improvements.

Monitoring, measurement, analysis and evaluation is focused on gathering evidence throughout the quality management cycle. The monitoring and measurement phases are conducted as part of other processes, all the way from initial design planning through to customer feedback and on the QMS generally. This data is then analysed and evaluated to determine whether the product or service, and QMS, is meeting its quality requirements and the organisation's quality objectives.

To properly establish this process, the organisation needs to be sure that it has activities and processes in place to gather the appropriate information. This information should be pushed through a rigorous procedure to make certain that it is then assessed and acted upon, and that the outputs of the procedure are passed to appropriate management, with summaries being fed into the management review.

Internal audits are a different matter. For organisations without any previous experience conducting internal management system audits, some training may be invaluable.[10] It is also worth securing a copy of ISO19011 *Guidelines for auditing management systems*, which is recommended as guidance in a note to Subclause 9.2.3.

Whereas monitoring and measurement is conducted continually, internal audits are planned assessments that focus on the functioning of the QMS, its conformity with the organisation's own requirements and those of ISO 9001. Internal management system audits normally involve interviews with key personnel (process owners, for instance) and the gathering and review of evidence (documented, observed and/or verbally reported) in

---

[10] Training providers can deliver certificated qualifications that can be completed relatively quickly – usually within a couple of days.

order to determine whether the quality management processes are being carried out as defined and meet requirements. As before, where nonconformities exist they should be identified and acted upon by the appropriate management. Audit results are also passed along to the management review.

The management review is the process by which the organisation's top management formally assesses the QMS and determines any necessary changes. The Standard lays out clear guidance for the inputs to the review, as well as defining the sort of actions that should result as outputs.

Clause 10 – Improvement

Improving the QMS is a core requirement of ISO 9001 because improving the processes that govern quality management will naturally improve the quality of products and services.

Subclause 10.1 sets out the kinds of actions that the organisation can take to improve the QMS and the products and services. The note to the subclause provides examples of the sorts of improvements that can occur, which helpfully includes things like innovation and reorganisation. This highlights that the QMS can be improved by processes that originate outside of its scope.

Nonconformity and corrective actions are covered in Subclause 10.2

The Standard sets a number of requirements for nonconformities and corrective actions, but these needn't be as distinct and bureaucratic as it may appear. Rather, your method should focus on reacting to the nonconformity once it is identified, evaluating the need for action to address the root cause and other occurrences of the same issue, applying the determined treatment(s), reviewing the effectiveness of any treatment(s), considering the effect on risks and opportunities and, of course, updating the QMS if necessary. This can be handled relatively simply and is really just a reiteration of the methods most competent people would use anyway.

The final subclause in the Standard is a clear statement of the requirement for continual improvement. It is useful to note the distinction between 'continual' and 'continuous' to avoid headaches in the future:

- Continual means that it recurs regularly; it is something that is repeated frequently.
- Continuous means that it occurs without interruption.

Although many people use the terms interchangeably, the organisation must make sure that it continually examines opportunities for improvement (to both the QMS and to quality in general) and implements those that are viable.

CHAPTER 6: CERTIFICATION

The journey to certification can take some time, depending on how large or complex your scoped organisation is. In general, larger organisations can reach certification in about eight to twelve months, whereas smaller companies can obviously achieve this somewhat faster – in the extreme in as little as two months. This is the time between deciding that you wish to pursue ISO 9001 and achieving certification.[11]

Once your organisation has actually implemented its QMS in accordance with the Standard, there are a few final steps worth taking before booking your certification audit:

- Get the QMS running
  Once all the pieces are in place, you should have schedules set up for the regular elements like monitoring and measurement, internal QMS audits and management reviews. Without these in place and proof that they're working, it's difficult to prove that your QMS actually meets the Standard's requirements. You don't need to have a year's data to prove this, but some records of initial quality measurements and audits, evidence that you have assessed any nonconformities that might have occurred, and an effective continual improvement process (shown in records of management reviews, for instance) will go a long way to proving that the QMS is a functioning management system

---

[11] Different certification bodies and service providers quote varying lengths from initial commitment to quality management through to certification, but the preceding estimates are generally representative. Furthermore, as ISO 9001:2015 is very new at the time of writing, these numbers are based on implementing ISO 9001:2008. It's reasonable to assume that the length of the process will not be markedly different under the 2015 version of the Standard.

rather than a static 'snapshot' of what a QMS might look like.

Remember: having documented processes doesn't prove they're being followed. Having records of the processes working as described *is* proof that they are being followed (but interviews and observation by an independent auditor can also demonstrate proof).

- Gap analysis

  As mentioned earlier, a gap analysis is a good method to use early in the implementation to see where your organisation stands, but it's equally useful once you think you've got everything in place. Even if your QMS appears to be functioning correctly, it's a good idea to make sure that every requirement is being met.

- Pre-certification audit

  Ideally this would be separate from your internal QMS audit regime to make sure you have external validation. Whether it involves getting someone from another part of the organisation to audit the QMS or engaging a consultant to do it for you, it will help prepare you for the audit as well as identifying any oversights. In general, it's more useful to have an external party perform this audit, as they are less likely to be influenced by personal relationships or organisational politics, and are better positioned to provide a truly objective review.

Assuming the results of the gap analysis and pre-certification audit are positive, your organisation will be ready for certification.

Even with these preparations made, certifying your QMS can be a daunting prospect. This is especially true for smaller organisations that may feel they do not have the resources available to have a 'proper' management system in place, so it's important to dispel a few myths about certification.

Do I have to certify?

Although certification is definitely valuable, some organisations may feel it's unnecessary and that simply conforming to the Standard is sufficient. This is entirely true – many benefits are derived solely from implementing good practice quality management. If you're happy simply gaining these benefits and are not too terribly worried about being able to demonstrate your credentials, then conformance may be enough.

Certification is an expensive disruption

Certification need not be expensive because the length of the certification audit scales with the size of your organisation, so smaller businesses can generally be audited in just a few days and, hence, relatively inexpensively. Naturally, larger organisations with more products and services, and more complex processes, will take longer, but are equally likely to gain more by being certified (such as access to new markets, clients and so on).

There's so much documentation involved

In reality, there's only as much documentation as you need. Many organisations make the mistake of thinking that *literally everything* has to be documented, which results in a mess of documentation and little coherence. For small organisations in particular, you should be wary of creating too many policies, procedures and work instructions. Rather, make sure you have enough documentation to tell people how the process works (a work instruction for the product/service and for checking the product/service) where it is needed and to check that they're doing it correctly (such as a log or checklist). If a process is suitably controlled and measured to ensure it is systematically communicated, understood, executed and effective so as to be repeatable and dependable without fully documenting it then, in the absence of an explicit requirement for it to be documented, you do not need to write it down.

Certification won't guarantee quality

It's true that a certified QMS won't guarantee quality – because nothing can make that guarantee. What certification *does* guarantee is that your organisation is doing everything it can to ensure quality and minimise customer dissatisfaction. Furthermore, because the QMS is inherently a preventive action, certification shows that your organisation is proactive in meeting customer requirements.

Can't my customers audit my quality processes instead of paying for a certification body?

Although some customers will be happy to do that, many more don't want to spend the time auditing a host of suppliers individually. Furthermore, if you have several customers who all want validation of your quality credentials, then repeated audits by your customers is likely to become a significant burden and disruption. Because ISO 9001 is the internationally recognised standard for quality management, being certified means that the majority of your customers will be perfectly happy with seeing the certificate and checking that the scope of your QMS (stated on the certificate) covers your relationship with them. This means that all of those customer audits can be replaced by a single certification audit, with less extensive surveillance audits annually in most cases through to the three-year recertification audit.

The certification auditor is just looking for problems

This is only true if you have a very bad auditor. Certification Body auditors are passionate about quality management and, like anyone passionate about something, they want to see it done right. If you establish a good relationship with your certification auditor, you'll find that their reporting can be very helpful in providing opportunities for improvement and addressing nonconformities.

Maintaining quality

Although a certification to ISO 9001:2015 is proof that your organisation has implemented a management system that conforms to the specification, it is not proof that your organisation continues to follow best practice. Furthermore, your certification body will want to conduct surveillance audits at least annually, and organisations that don't make much of an effort to continue running their QMS will generally find it much, much harder to negotiate their next certification body audit without significant findings being raised and ultimately jeopardising certification.

Mercifully, the whole process is actually very simple if the QMS has been properly established. The critical stage is making sure that you select an appropriate process approach, such as the plan-do-check-act cycle.

Regardless of the methodology you choose to follow, you should be sure that it has a cyclical structure so that it continues working without requiring additional impetus.

ISO 9001 RESOURCES

IT Governance has many years' experience helping organisations implement ISO 9001 and achieve certification. We have a range of products and services covering the whole process of implementation, all the way through certification and beyond.

Green papers

Green papers are brief articles discussing a single topic in depth. Written by practising experts in their fields, the green papers offer valuable insights, completely free of charge.

www.itgovernance.co.uk/green-papers.aspx

Transition tools

For organisations updating their QMS from 2008 to 2015, we have several useful products to help ease the transition process.

ISO 9001:2008 to ISO 9001:2015 Conversion Tool

This tool aims to identify the changes to ISO 9001:2015 and to provide guidance on adapting an existing ISO 9001:2008-compliant QMS into an ISO 9001:2015-compliant QMS. It includes a summary of the key changes, descriptions of the notable retentions, an outline of the new requirements for documented information, and a complete structure mapping that highlights how the two standards relate.

www.itgovernance.co.uk/shop/p-1785-iso-9001-2008-to-iso-9001-2015-conversion-tool.aspx

ISO 9001:2008 to ISO 9001:2015 Gap Analysis Tool

The ISO 9001:2008 to ISO 9001:2015 Gap Analysis Tool has been created to help organisations that have implemented an ISO 9001:2008-compliant QMS to assess their current compliance against the Standard, ISO 9001:2015. The ISO 9001:2008 to ISO 9001:2015 Gap Analysis Tool will help organisations prioritise their workload and initial project planning and prepare for a final, pre-certification audit review of their QMS.

www.itgovernance.co.uk/shop/p-1729-iso9001-2008-to-iso-9001-2015-gap-analysis-tool.aspx

Gap analysis

Gap analysis tools are used to identify the differences between what you currently do and what the Standard requires. They usually present a series of yes/no questions that allow you to identify where you need to assign your resources to comply with the Standard.

ISO 9001:2015 Gap Analysis Tool

This ISO 9001:2015 Gap Analysis Tool has been created to help organisations identify where they are – and are not – meeting the requirements of ISO 9001. This self-assessment gap analysis tool provides a clear, colour-coded, control-by-control report on the high-level general state of organisational compliance with ISO 9001:2015.

The results and the analysis that this tool provides is the basis for organisations then to conduct a detailed, granular assessment of their current QMS. This tool is particularly useful for organisations tackling a QMS for the first time. It provides clear direction for project managers identifying where they need to start.

http://www.itgovernance.co.uk/shop/p-1820-iso-9001-2015-iso9001-2015-gap-analysis-tool.aspx

Documentation toolkits

Documentation toolkits provide pre-written documents and templates to let you quickly fulfil management system documentation requirements. Although some work is still involved to make sure the documentation reflects what your organisation actually does, it considerably speeds up the documentation process and provides a ready-made document structure.

ISO Project Initiation Documentation (PID) Toolkit

This documentation toolkit helps you to identify the necessary steps in your ISO management system implementation, helping you establish a sound base for your project before seeking Board-level commitment. Once these documents have been reviewed and approved, this toolkit will act as a base against which you can assess your project's progress, risks, issues, change and ongoing viability.

www.itgovernance.co.uk/shop/p-1789-iso-project-initiation-documentation-pid-toolkit.aspx

ISO 9001:2015 QMS Documentation Toolkit

The ISO 9001:2015 QMS Documentation Toolkit provides organisations of any size or type with pre-written templates that will save them time and money when implementing an ISO 9001:2015-compliant QMS. This toolkit contains the fundamental tools and material you need to easily start your QMS project and continuously support its implementation.

The toolkit features one-time information input to automatically populate documents with common information, a dashboard to keep track of the progress of your documentation, and the ISO 9001:2008 to ISO 9001:2015 Gap Analysis Tool. It also forms part of our integrated management system, which enables you to readily integrate your QMS with other management systems using our modular approach.

www.itgovernance.co.uk/shop/p-1259-iso9001-iso-9001-2015-quality-management-system-(qms)-documentation-toolkit.aspx

Consultancy

IT Governance consultants use methodologies and tools that have been developed and honed over ten years. Support options range from acting as a mentor and coach to your internal project team through to coming in and running the project for you. Either way, we focus on enabling a suitable transfer of skills and knowledge so that you can easily maintain your own QMS and ISO 9001 certification after your successful initial certification audit.

With our wide-ranging expertise across the entire management systems sphere, we can even identify linkages and improvements to drive business efficiency and bottom-line benefits through your whole operation.

www.itgovernance.co.uk/consulting.aspx

ITG RESOURCES

IT Governance Ltd sources, creates and delivers products and services to meet the real-world, evolving IT governance needs of today's organisations, directors, managers and practitioners.

The ITG website (*www.itgovernance.co.uk*) is the international one-stop-shop for corporate and IT governance information, advice, guidance, books, tools, training and consultancy. On the website you will find the following page related to the subject matter of this book:

www.itgovernance.co.uk/iso9001-quality-management-standards.aspx

Publishing Services

IT Governance Publishing (ITGP) is the world's leading IT-GRC publishing imprint that is wholly owned by IT Governance Ltd.

With books and tools covering all IT governance, risk and compliance frameworks, we are the publisher of choice for authors and distributors alike, producing unique and practical publications of the highest quality, in the latest formats available, which readers will find invaluable.

www.itgovernancepublishing.co.uk is the website dedicated to ITGP. Other titles published by ITGP that may be of interest include:

- Exploding the Myths Surrounding ISO9000

  www.itgovernance.co.uk/shop/p-1292.aspx

- A Guide to Effective Internal Management System Audits

  www.itgovernance.co.uk/shop/p-1542.aspx

- Fundamentals of Information Risk Management Auditing

  www.itgovernance.co.uk/shop/p-1814.aspx

We also offer a range of off-the-shelf *toolkits* that give comprehensive, customisable documents to help users create the specific documentation they need to properly implement a management system or standard. Written by experienced practitioners and based on the latest best practice, ITGP toolkits can save months of work for organisations working towards compliance with a given standard.

Please visit *www.itgovernance.co.uk/shop/c-129-toolkits.aspx* to see our full range of toolkits.

Books and tools published by IT Governance Publishing (ITGP) are available from all business booksellers and the following websites:

www.itgovernance.eu   *www.itgovernanceusa.com*

www.itgovernance.in   *www.itgovernancesa.co.za*

www.itgovernance.asia.

Training Services

Thanks to Annex SL – the high-level structure common to all new ISO standards – an ISO 9001:2015-compliant QMS is now fully integrable with management systems based on other ISO standards, such as ISO 27001, which sets out the specifications for an information security management system (ISMS). This means that creating an integrated management system that addresses your quality management and information security concerns is now easier than ever before. If you're a compliance manager, or have been tasked with implementing management systems standards to create greater business efficiency, you may be interested in IT Governance's ISO 27001 Learning Pathway.

Many courses are available in Live Online as well as classroom formats, so delegates can learn and achieve essential career progression from the comfort of their own homes and offices.

For information on any of our courses, including PCI DSS compliance, business continuity, IT governance, service management and professional certification courses, please see: *www.itgovernance.co.uk/ training.aspx*

Professional Services and Consultancy

ISO 9001, the international standard for quality management, sets out the requirements for a quality management system (QMS), a best-practice approach to quality management that can be used by organisations of all types and sizes in any location, irrespective of the products and services they provide.

Implementing, maintaining and continually improving a QMS can be daunting. Fortunately, IT Governance offers a comprehensive range of flexible, practical consultancy packages to help any organisation to implement a QMS and achieve certification to ISO 9001, using methodologies and tools that have been developed and honed over 10 years.

For more information on our ISO 9001 consultancy service, please see: *www.itgovernance.co.uk/iso-9001-quality-management-consultancy.aspx*

For general information about our other consultancy services, including for ISO 20000, ISO 22301, ISO 27001, Cyber Essentials, the PCI DSS, Data Protection and more, please see: *www.itgovernance.co.uk/consulting.aspx*

Newsletter

You can stay up to date with the latest developments across the whole spectrum of IT governance subject matter, including risk management, information security, ITIL and IT service management, project governance, compliance and so much more, by subscribing to our newsletter.

Simply visit our subscription centre and select your preferences:

www.itgovernance.co.uk/newsletter.aspx.

EU for product safety is Stephen Evans, The Mill Enterprise Hub, Stagreenan, Drogheda, Co. Louth, A92 CD3D, Ireland. (servicecentre@itgovernance.eu)

www.ingramcontent.com/pod-product-compliance
Lightning Source LLC
Chambersburg PA
CBHW070900070326
40690CB00009B/1927